W9-AKB-756

DALE
EARNHARDT

DALE EARNHARDT

A. R. McHUGH

THE CHILD'S WORLD®, INC.

ON THE COVER...

Front cover: Dale waits in his car during a break in the action of the 1998 Daytona 500.
Page 2: Dale stays ahead of the pack during the 1995 Miller Genuine Draft 500.

Published in the United States of America by The Child's World®, Inc.
PO Box 326
Chanhassen, MN 55317-0326
800-599-READ
www.childsworld.com

Product Manager Mary Berendes
Editor Katherine Stevenson
Designer Mary Berendes
Contributor Bob Temple

Photo Credits
© AP/WideWorld Photos: 10, 13, 15, 19
© Brian Spurlock/SportsChrome-USA: 22
© Evan Pinkus/SportsChrome-USA: cover, 16
© Greg Crisp/SportsChrome-USA: 2, 6, 9
© Reuters NewMedia Inc./CORBIS: 20

Library of Congress Cataloging-in-Publication Data
McHugh, A. R.
Dale Earnhardt / by A.R. McHugh.
p. cm.
Includes index.
ISBN 1-56766-966-2
1. Earnhardt, Dale, 1951-—Juvenile literature.
2. Automobile racing drivers—United States—Biography—Juvenile literature.
[1. Earnhardt, Dale, 1951- . 2. Automobile racing drivers.] I. Title.
GV1032.E18 M34 2001
796.72'092—dc21

00-011886

TABLE OF CONTENTS

BORN TO RACE

"Vroom! Vroom!" That's the sound of a teenager racing his car on the country roads of North Carolina. The boy was named Dale Earnhardt. He was born on a farm in Kannapolis, North Carolina. His father, Ralph, raced cars when Dale was young. When Dale learned to drive, his father taught him how to race. Dale started racing in towns near where he lived. He kept getting better and better. His father cheered him on, but in 1973, his father died while repairing a car. Would Dale keep on racing?

Yes! He kept racing and winning. Two years later he raced in his first big race, the World 600. Did he win? No. He finished 22nd. He then raced in eight big races over the next three years. In 1979 he got a chance to show how good he really was. He was picked to drive for a racing team headed by Rod Osterlund. Dale got to drive a better, faster car. He also had a good crew of **mechanics** to keep the car running fast and fix any problems. Dale raced a car with the #3 on it. He did well and was named Rookie of the Year, which meant he was the best new driver. Would Dale keep on winning? That's what the racing world was waiting to see.

Dale's famous #3 car speeds along the track during the 1999 Goody's Body Pain 500.

TO BE A RACE CAR DRIVER

Racing is hard work. It takes a whole team to race. Dale is the driver of the car, but he couldn't race without his team. His team is made up of people who help in many ways. Some work as mechanics and fix the car if it breaks down. A spotter watches the race and tells Dale where the other cars are. Other team members use stopwatches, **walkie-talkies**, and computers to help Dale drive during the race.

Some of Dale's team members work in the **pit** during a race. The pit is the area on the inside of the racetrack where the race car goes when there's trouble. The team members who work in the pit are called the **pit crew**. Dale and the pit crew chief talk on their walkie-talkies when Dale is about to make a **pit stop**. A pit stop has to be fast, or the racer will fall behind the other cars. When Dale makes a pit stop, one person fills up the car with gas. Another wipes the windshield clean. Others jack up the car and change the tires. There's even one person whose job is to give Dale a drink of water! If there are no problems, the pit crew can get Dale's car back on the racetrack within 15 seconds. If something on the car breaks down, the pit crew mechanics must fix it fast! If they can't get it fixed, the car is out of the race.

Dale's pit crew quickly tends to his car during the 1995 Bud at the Glen race.

THE WINSTON CUP

After Dale was Rookie of the Year, he kept racing well. He raced against famous drivers such as Richard Petty and Cale Yarlborough. Dale competed in a racing league called NASCAR, the National Association of Stock Car Auto Racing. NASCAR keeps track of how each racer does in every race. The racers get points for doing well. At the end of the year, a prize is given to the driver with the most points. This prize is called the Winston Cup. By the end of 1980, Dale had the most points of any racer. Dale had won the Winston Cup!

SPEED

Race cars are built for speed and use special gas. Mechanics prepare the engine to go as fast as possible. In fact, Dale's car can race at 190 miles per hour. That's almost three times as fast as drivers can drive on the highway! Dale wears a helmet with a walkie-talkie in it. He wears gloves and a fireproof body suit. The car has special seat belts and is **reinforced** to protect Dale in case of a crash. It even has a fire extinguisher in case there's a fire.

Dale's car (#3) slides upside down after flipping over during the 1997 Daytona 500.

NASCAR has rules to make racing as safe as possible. Even so, accidents sometimes happen. Even something as simple as a flat tire can cause a crash. Dale has been in many crashes. His car has smashed up against the wall of the racetrack. In one crash he broke his collarbone and his **sternum.** Another time he broke his leg. In 1999 he had to have back surgery because of racing injuries.

THE INTIMIDATOR

When Dale races, he races hard and fast. Sometimes he drives his car very close to other cars and passes them. He is so good at passing and winning that other racers began to call him the "Intimidator." Even though he is so good at winning, he shakes other drivers' hands after each race. By doing this, he shows his good **sportsmanship.**

Of all the **professional** auto racers, Dale was the leading prizewinner in four of the last ten years. He finished nine out of every ten races—a better record than any other current racer. This record means that he crashed or broke down less often than anybody else. It also shows how good he and his crew are. He is so good that he has won the Winston Cup seven times.

Dale holds his chest as he climbs out of his car after practice laps for the 1996 Bud at the Glen Winston Cup race. He had broken his collarbone and sternum in a crash two weeks earlier.

THE DAYTONA 500

Over the years, Dale and his #3 car had won every big race at least once—except the Daytona 500. The Daytona 500 is the biggest NASCAR race of the year. It's held in Daytona Beach, Florida, and all the best drivers come out to race. In 19 years, Dale had never won it. It seemed as if every time Dale entered that race, his car broke down, crashed, or kept getting passed by other cars. One time he was winning but got a flat tire. Another time he ran out of gas when he was in the lead.

On February 15, 1998, Dale was going to race in his twentieth Daytona 500. His car ran well in practice, and Dale knew he had a good pit crew. Could the Intimidator win the race this time?

THE INSPIRATIONAL PENNY

Before the race, a five-year-old girl visited Dale. Her name was Wessa Miller, and she was in a wheelchair. She said her biggest dream was to meet Dale Earnhardt and watch him race in the Daytona 500. A group called the Make-A-Wish Foundation arranged for her to go to the race and meet Dale. Wessa gave Dale a penny and wished him luck. Dale had his pit crew tape the penny to the inside of his car so he could see it while driving in the race.

Dale heads toward the first turn at the 1998 Daytona 500.

"I met a little girl on Saturday. She has to stay in a wheelchair. But she was not worried about a thing," said Dale. "She was laughing and smiling and happy—not concerned about anything. She said, 'I rubbed this lucky penny and it's going to win you the Daytona 500. It's your race.'"

Wessa Miller and over 100,000 other fans filled the stadium and watched the race. Each driver had to go 200 **laps** around the track to finish this 500-mile-long race. Great drivers such as Jeff Gordon, Mark Martin, and Bobby Labonte were also in the race. Bobby Labonte got to start the race in front of Dale and the other cars. After the start, Dale quickly started passing other cars and moving up. He took the lead and held it most of the way. But by the time the race was more than half over, Dale had lost the lead. Could he get it back and win?

A TOUGH FINISH

On lap 140, Dale passed racer Mike Skinner to take the lead again. On lap 174 there was an accident, so Dale and the other leaders went into the pits to get more gas and change tires. Dale's pit crew was the fastest, and Dale was the first racer back onto the track. Skinner, Labonte, and some other racers were right behind. Dale held the lead until lap 199, when there was another wreck. All the cars had to slow down with just one lap to go. Could Dale hold his lead? The drivers zoomed around the final turn, and Dale crossed the finish line first. The Intimidator had won!

Dale zooms across the finish line during the 1998 Daytona 500.

After Dale won, the crowd jumped to its feet and cheered. Dale drove his car to Victory Lane to get the championship trophy. All the other pit crews lined up to watch and cheer. Dale and his own pit crew jumped for joy. "Yes! Yes! Yes!" Dale shouted. "Twenty years! Can you believe it! The Daytona 500 is over, and we won it. We won it!"

Driver Mark Martin commented, "He's the best I've ever come up against." Dale said, "This was one of the most awesome races I've ever won. It's a great feeling every race car driver wants to feel and deserves to feel after all the hard work they go through."

Dale also said, "I have had a lot of great fans and people behind me all through the years and I just can't thank them enough." And what about the lucky penny? Dale said, "All race fans are special, but a little girl like that—that's in a wheelchair—that life has not been good to, giving [me] a penny and wishing [me] luck, that's pretty special.... Inspiration is what it's all about.... Determination and having a never-say-die attitude—never giving up—those are keys to achieving success.... I put that penny on the dashboard and it's still on the dashboard."

Dale celebrates as he jumps out of his car in Victory Lane after winning the 1998 Daytona 500.

A FAMILY RACING TOWARD THE FUTURE

Dale has four children, Dale Jr., Kerry, Kelley, and Taylor. Dale Jr. and Kerry are both race car drivers, too. Dale Jr. is nicknamed "Little E" and Kerry is "Middle E." "Look at all my kids—I'm pretty proud of all of them," Dale said. "All of them did the right thing in life."

Some people think Dale Earnhart is too old to keep racing. They think he should just let his children race instead. But he keeps on racing and winning. If you ever watch the Intimidator race, you just might see him and his #3 car in Victory Lane!

Dale celebrates as he holds the trophy after winning a 2000 IROC race.

TIMELINE

April 29, 1951	Dale Earnhardt is born in Kannapolis, North Carolina.
1975	Dale races in his first big race, the World 600.
1979	Dale wins the Rookie of the Year Award.
1980	Dale wins his first Winston Cup.
1986	Dale wins his second Winston Cup.
1987	Dale wins his third Winston Cup.
1990	Dale wins his fourth Winston Cup. He also wins the IROC Championship.
1991	Dale wins his fifth Winston Cup.
1993	Dale wins his sixth Winston Cup.
1994	Dale wins his seventh Winston Cup.
1995	Dale wins the IROC Championship for the second time.
1998	Dale finally wins the Daytona 500.
1999	Dale wins the IROC Championship for the third time.
2000	Dale wins the IROC Championship for the fourth time.

Dale poses for photographers as he holds
the 2000 IROC Championship trophy.

GLOSSARY

laps (LAPS)
In racing, a lap is one trip around the racetrack. The Daytona 500 is a 200-lap race.

mechanics (meh-KAN-iks)
Mechanics are people who fix machines. Dale Earnhardt has many mechanics who work on his car.

pit (PIT)
In racing, the pit is the area on the inside of a racetrack. During a race, Dale Earnhardt drives his car to the pit to fill it with gas or make repairs.

pit crew (PIT KREW)
The pit crew is the team of mechanics and other people who work in the pit. Dale Earnhardt has a very good pit crew.

pit stop (PIT STOP)
A race car makes a pit stop when it pulls into the pit to get gas or make repairs. Dale Earnhardt makes many pit stops during every race.

professional (proh-FESH-un-ull)
In sports, a professional is good enough to earn money doing something most people do only for fun. Dale Earnhardt, Jeff Gordon, and Bobby Labonte are professional race car drivers.

reinforced (ree-in-FORST)
When something is reinforced, it is made stronger. The inside of Dale Earnhardt's car is reinforced to help protect Dale in case of a crash.

sportsmanship (SPORTS-man-ship)
Good sportsmanship means playing fair and behaving well toward other players. Dale Earnhardt shows good sportsmanship in his racing.

sternum (STER-num)
The sternum is the breastbone, the bone in the middle of the chest that protects the heart. Dale broke his sternum in a crash.

walkie-talkies (WAWK-ee TAWK-eez)
Walkie-talkies are small radios that let people talk to each other over short distances. Dale Earnhardt has a walkie-talkie in his helmet to talk with his pit crew during a race.

INDEX

JB
B
E arnhard Dale Earnhardt.
t
M

McHugh, A. Rose.

DATE			